# 10 RULES TO ENTREPRENEURSHIP

*Answer Your Call, Live Your Dream*

by

**James B. Kynes, Jr.**

edited by
Dispersions

10 Rules to Entrepreneurship, Answer Your Call,
Live Your Dream - 1st U.S. ed.

ISBN-978-0-9855286-6-9 (paperback)

# Table of Contents

*This book is your guide to the journey of entrepreneurship. Inside, you'll find key steps to help you achieve your dream of successful entrepreneurship.*

# Foreword

By J. Bernard Ma'at Kynes

***10 Rules to Entrepreneurship: Answer Your Call, Live Your Dream*** is an excellently written book that offers an integrative approach towards self-actualization on the one hand, and an aspect of spiritual consciousness as a business model on the other. James captures more than simply *Rules to Entrepreneurship*, which presents the "do's and don'ts" in the business process. He also outlines a path for readers to discover more of their inner core, while becoming successful entrepreneurs in today's marketplace.

To reach a higher state of being is a lifelong journey and process, that can lead to a fuller realization of one's personal and professional aspirations. The 10 rules will assist in the development of your potential as a business leader, while directly and indirectly providing a guide to entrepreneurship.

To *Answer Your Call* is more than choosing a profession, career or job simply for the purpose of earning money. James has connected the spirituality of being an entrepreneur with what I call *soulful integrity*; this implies a *vocational* aspiration at one's core. Living your dream is in essence, honoring your call from a higher source—spiritual consciousness.

Who then benefits from these *10 Rules to Entrepreneurship*? The entrepreneurs who are following their calling, living the dream, and those with whom they encounter on their journey. In short, throughout this process the more important element being developed is the relationship—*positive projective energy*!

Consequently, within the business circle, everyone's life moves to a higher level on the self-actualization and spiritual consciousness interplay. They answer their unique calling with courage, commitment and compassion while simultaneously living their dreams!

Therefore, the ***10 Rules to Entrepreneurship: Answer Your Call, Live Your Dream*** is an excellent guide for those honoring their call to live as an entrepreneur in any business industry, including commercial real estate.

We thank the author of this book, James, my beloved son, for his many years of dedicated work and experience in his business endeavors. He has written not only from his head, but also from his heart through the personal journey of his own blood, sweat and tears!  As his father and friend, I have observed his determination and dedicated heart and mind, as he offers these *10 rules to Entrepreneurship* to the reader.

# Chapter 1

## Answering the Call

We start with the foundation—the call that pulls you toward something greater, a purpose that resonates deeply within you. For many, this calling feels like an inner pull, sometimes conflicting with current circumstances but never fading. Here, we'll explore what it means to recognize and answer that call.

### Recognizing the Call

Think back to your early years. Our purpose often emerges in childhood or adolescence, disguised as a hobby or interest. Perhaps there was something you were passionate about, but you never thought it could lead to a career. Many of us get caught up in the traditional path— college, a degree, a "safe" job. And eventually, we wonder, is this really what I'm meant to do?

Answering a calling isn't always a clear-cut decision. It's a process of growth and spiritual discovery. Circumstances, challenges, and even setbacks often become the guiding forces that help you recognize the purpose pulling at you.

### A Personal Story of My Call

For me, this moment of clarity came when I was working with a business management firm in a role that seemed like a dream job. I was recruiting athletes and helping manage their business portfolios—exactly what I thought I wanted to do. But even as I found success, something didn't feel right.

One day, in a moment of frustration, I asked, "What should I be doing?" Almost as if in answer, a voice nudged me toward a barbershop. I resisted at first, thinking it was a step backward. But that persistent pull wouldn't let go, and I finally gave in. Looking back, I realize that listening to this call opened doors I hadn't imagined. It led me into a career that allowed me to impact others in meaningful ways.

**Connecting Back to Your Journey**

As you read this, think about your own journey. Have you ever felt drawn to something that didn't fit your plans? Recognizing a calling often means letting go of a path that seems "secure" in favor of a path that feels right. The purpose you're called to fulfill won't always make sense at first, but it's there to guide you.

**Key Takeaway: Embrace the Call**

Once you engage with your calling, life changes in unexpected ways. Challenges arise, but they are part of the journey. Being open to growth and adapting to the lessons life brings you is essential for nurturing your calling. Remember, humility and resilience are the foundations of true success.

**Chapter 1 - Answering the Call Summary**

*The process of growth and discovery.*

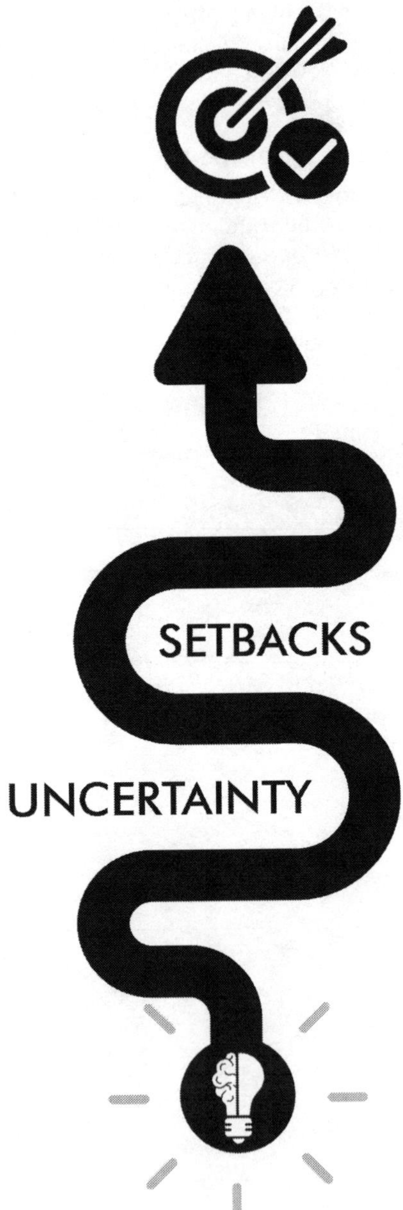

# Chapter 2

## Creating a Sound Business Plan

A well-constructed business plan is your roadmap—a guide to keep you aligned with your goals and the steps necessary to achieve them. This plan brings clarity to your vision and serves as a valuable tool for decision-making along the way.

### Flexibility in Your Business Plan

While a business plan provides structure, it's crucial to stay adaptable. The market, your goals, and the needs of your business will evolve. Embrace flexibility so your plan can grow with you. I've found that remaining open to adjustments, even minor ones, often leads to new opportunities.

### Pros and Cons of Starting with a Business Plan

Creating a business plan at the outset has clear benefits, and there are common approaches.

Pros: It forces you to research, understand your competition, and prepare for challenges.

Cons: Some find that spending too much time planning can delay action or lead to overthinking.

Whether you start with a detailed plan or learn as you go, the goal is to have a strong foundation. I recommend beginning with research on your industry and the basics of running a business, even if your plan isn't finalized.

### Crafting a Plan That Works for You

Begin by writing down your concept or idea. Make an outline of what you know and areas you need to research. Seek advice from people with experience in your field and remember that your vision is unique to you. Include these essentials in your plan:

1. Mission Statement: This should be a concise statement reflecting the purpose of your business.

2. Vision Statement: This complements the mission, giving a clear picture of what success looks like.

3. Executive Summary: A brief overview of the business, outlining costs, projected returns, and the overall impact.

**A Research Starter Kit**

If you're new to business planning, here are a few tools to get you started:

- Industry research reports (such as, IBISWorld or Statista)
- Competitor analysis (free tools such as, Similarweb or Google Trends)
- Customer feedback surveys (such as, SurveyMonkey or Typeform)

**Key Takeaway: A Living Document**

Your business plan is a living document—it's there to provide direction, but can evolve as you grow. Remember, a strong plan gives you clarity and adaptability, helping you navigate challenges while staying focused on your goals.

## Chapter 2 - Business Plan Summary

*Your business plan is your roadmap to success.*

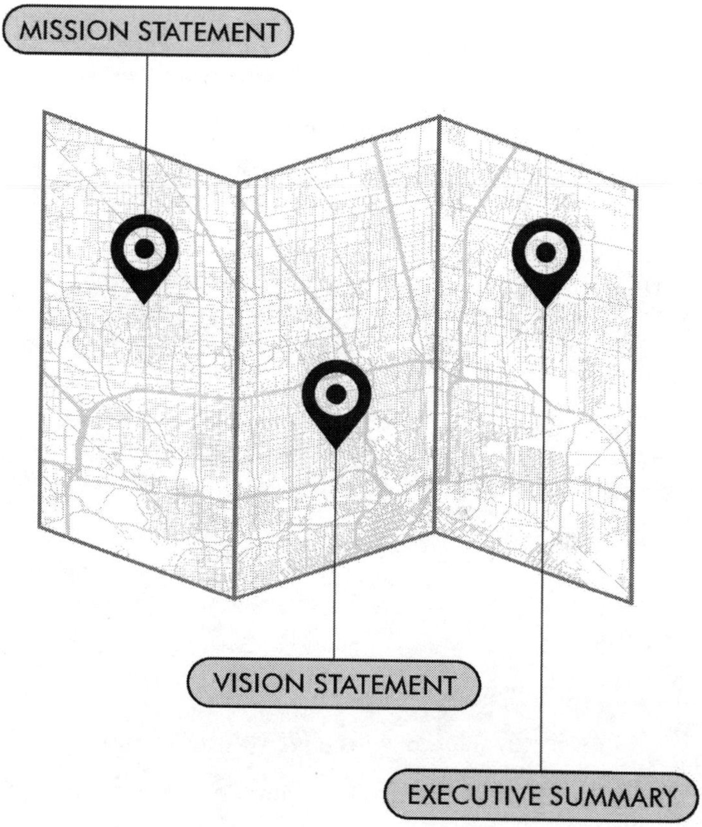

# Chapter 3

## Identifying the Team

Building a successful business requires a strong, aligned team. Identifying the right people to support your vision will help you avoid costly mistakes, and create a foundation for long-term growth.

### Dream Killers vs. Good Mentors

When choosing who to have around you, it's essential to distinguish between those who uplift and those who may unintentionally undermine your vision.

Dream Killers often discourage your ideas, either out of fear or from a place of personal limitation. For instance, someone who hasn't pursued their own dreams might suggest that yours are unrealistic.

Good Mentors, on the other hand, see your potential. They guide you towards growth, offering valuable feedback and sometimes challenging you to think deeper.

### Checklist for Team Selection

When evaluating potential team members or advisors, use this checklist to ensure they're aligned with your vision:

- Do they challenge you constructively?
- Are they aligned with your values and goals?
- Do they bring skills that complement your own?

### Self-Reflection on Leadership

Your team reflects your leadership. Take a moment to consider: What role do I play in motivating my team? How do I support their growth and align them with my goals? Effective leaders create an environment that inspires others to perform at their best.

### The Right Fit for Your Team

Consider the specific qualities you need in each role, from leaders to customer-facing roles and behind-the-scenes support. Building a balanced team means finding individuals who not only possess the necessary skills, but also share a commitment to your mission.

### Key Takeaway: Cultivating Connections

Invest time in building authentic, mutually beneficial relationships. The right team doesn't just come together by chance—it's cultivated through trust, shared goals, and a dedication to the vision. Surround yourself with people who uplift, challenge, and support your journey.

## Chapter 3 - Team Summary

*Identify the right people to support your vision.*

- Trust
- Shared goals
- Dedication to the vision

# Chapter 4

## Branding

Branding is more than a logo or a tagline, it's the core identity of your business. It's what sets you apart in the market and communicates your values to your audience. Building a strong brand is essential for lasting success.

### Personal Branding as a Foundation

Your personal brand is at the heart of your business brand. Reflect on what you stand for, what values you bring to your business, and how you want others to perceive you. For me, my personal brand has always been about integrity, quality, and dedication, which naturally extends to my business.

### Differentiating Brand Identity and Marketing

Branding defines "who you are" and "what you stand for." Marketing, on the other hand, is "how you communicate who you are." Building a clear brand identity helps to ensure that your marketing efforts are aligned and consistent.

### Defining Your Brand: A Step-by-Step Exercise

To help you establish a clear brand identity, try this quick exercise:

- Three Words: Write down three words you want people to associate with your brand.
- Brand Feel: Think about what feeling you want clients to have when they interact with your business.
- Visual Elements: Sketch or list elements that visually represent your brand, like colors, fonts, or symbols that align with your message.

## The Power of Brand Loyalty

When you invest in building a brand that resonates with people, you create brand loyalists— clients who believe in what you stand for. These loyal clients become advocates, spreading positive word-of-mouth testimonies and helping your business grow organically.

## Key Takeaway: Build a Brand That Lasts

Your brand is an investment in long-term success. It's a tool that builds trust, attracts the right audience, and creates a legacy for your business. Remember, branding is not just about standing out; it's about creating a lasting impression that aligns with your vision.

**Chapter 4 - Branding Summary**

*Branding, the core identity of your business, creates a lasting impression when aligned with your vision.*

# Chapter 5
## Partnership

Strategic partnerships can elevate your business by combining strengths and resources, but they must be approached with intention. A strong partnership is built on trust, complementary skills, and a shared vision.

### Understanding Your Value Proposition

Before seeking a partner, take a moment to identify your own value proposition. Ask yourself: What skills, experience, or resources do I bring to the table? Knowing your unique strengths helps you find a partner who complements rather than duplicates your abilities.

### Practical Tips for Vetting Potential Partners

When evaluating potential partners, consider these key aspects to ensure alignment:

- Shared Values: Do they share your core values and vision?
- Reliability: Have they shown commitment and follow-through in past projects?
- Transparency: Are they clear about their expectations and intentions?

### Good vs. Bad Partnerships Analogy

Just as in nature, partnerships in business have different dynamics. A lion and vulture can coexist, as each fulfills a role without interference. While a snake and a rodent represent a connection wherein one benefits at the other's expense. Choose partners who are like the lion and vulture—individuals who complement your skills and strengthen the business.

### Building Sustainable Partnerships

Long-term partnerships require effort,

communication, and patience. Avoid rushing into alliances out of desperation or convenience. Take time to understand your potential partner's strengths and motivations, thereby building a foundation of mutual respect and shared goals.

### Key Takeaway: Choose Wisely and Invest in Relationships

A solid partnership isn't just about shared resources; it's about shared growth and resilience. Invest in relationships that align with your vision, elevate your business, and contribute positively to your journey.

## Chapter 5 - Partnership Summary

*A strong partnership is built on trust, complementary skills and a shared vision.*

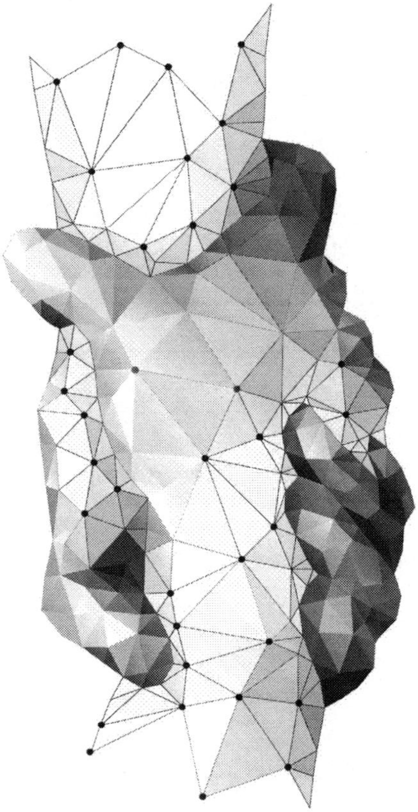

# Chapter 6

## Capital

Capital is the lifeblood of a business. Having access to funds—and knowing how to manage them—enables you to grow, overcome challenges, and take advantage of opportunities.

### Understanding Capital as More Than Funding

Capital isn't just money; it includes cash flow, credit, and assets that support your business. A strong financial foundation ensures stability, allowing you to make strategic decisions and weather fluctuations in the market.

### Financing Essentials

*Building a solid financial foundation starts with some key actions:*

- Establish a Financial Buffer: Aim to create an emergency fund to handle unexpected costs. Resourcefulness for Bootstrapping — utilizing personal funds or business revenue.

- Build a Relationship with Financial Advisors: Connect with a trusted advisor or banker who can guide you on financial matters and decisions.

- Track Cash Flow: Understanding your income and expenses is crucial for sustainability.

### Building Credit for Your Business

*Establishing business credit is an important step toward financial independence for your company. Here are some initial steps:*

- Obtain a DUNS Number: Register with Dun & Bradstreet to build a credit profile.

- Create Vendor Credit Lines: Many suppliers offer

credit terms for new businesses, helping you establish a positive credit history.

*Not everyone begins with significant capital. Consider alternatives:*

- Crowdfunding: Platforms like Kickstarter can help raise initial funds.
- Grants: Investigate small business grants for additional funding.
- Pre-Sales: Gauge interest and generate initial revenue by offering pre-sales of your product or service.

**Key Takeaway: Financial Discipline for Long-Term Success**

Capital is not only about securing funds, but also about using them wisely. Embrace financial discipline as a habit that will sustain you in the long run. Responsible money management enables you to grow, invest in opportunities, and keep your business on track.

## Chapter 6 - Capital Summary

*Build a solid financial foundation that will support your business.*

CASH FLOW + CREDIT + ASSETS

# Chapter 7

## Finding the Right Location

Location is one of the most critical choices in establishing a business. Your location affects visibility, accessibility, and the perception of your brand, all of which contribute to your success.

### Choosing a Location Based on Business Needs

*Not every business needs the same type of location. Here's a quick breakdown:*

- Retail and Service-Based Businesses:
  High-traffic areas benefit these businesses by maximizing visibility.

- Specialty or Appointment-Only Services:
  Private settings may work best, prioritizing client experience over visibility.

### Checklist for Working with Real Estate Consultants

*Partnering with a knowledgeable real estate consultant can make location selection easier. Use this checklist to find the right fit:*

- Commercial Real Estate Experience:
  Verify their expertise in commercial properties.

- Market Knowledge:
  Ensure they understand local trends, demographics, and zoning regulations.

- Budget Alignment:
  Discuss your budget and specific needs to avoid wasted time and misalignment.

### Tools for Analyzing Traffic Flow

Understanding traffic flow and visibility is essential for choosing a strategic location. Tools like Google Maps insights or commercial real estate software can provide data on foot traffic, drive-by visibility, and neighborhood demographics, helping you make an informed decision.

### Setting Realistic Growth Expectations

Finding a prime location is a major step, but success also requires time and a commitment to growth. As your business evolves, cultivating a loyal customer base takes patience. Don't expect overnight results. Instead, focus on building a strong presence over time.

### Key Takeaway: Strategic and Informed Location Selection

Your location should align with your business model, target market, and long-term vision. A well-chosen location enhances visibility, supports your brand, and provides a solid foundation for growth.

**Chapter 7 - Location Summary**

*Define your business needs when choosing a strategic location.*

RETAIL BUSINESS

SERVICE BASED BUSINESS

SPECIALTY SERVICES

APPOINTMENT ONLY SERVICES

# Chapter 8

## Marketing

Marketing is the engine that drives your brand to reach new audiences. It's about finding the best ways to connect with your target market, create awareness, and encourage loyalty.

### Mastering the Four P's

The "Four P's" are fundamental elements that shape your marketing approach:

- *Product:* Define what makes your product unique.
- *Price:* Set a price that aligns with your brand's positioning and target market.
- *Place:* Identify where your product is available and accessible to your audience.
- *Promotion:* Plan how to reach your audience effectively, from digital campaigns to in-person events.

### Crafting a Social Media Strategy

Social media is a powerful tool for connecting with clients. To create a strategy:

- Define Your Target Audience:
  Knowing who you're speaking to will help you tailor your messaging.
- Choose the Right Platforms:
  Each platform serves different purposes; choose those that align with your audience.
- Engage Consistently:
  A consistent presence builds recognition and trust. Consider creating a content calendar to stay organized.

### Consistency in Messaging

Your brand message should be clear, concise and consistent across all channels. Consistency not only builds trust but also strengthens brand identity, making it easier for clients to remember and relate to your business.

### Investing in Marketing as a Growth Tool

Marketing is an investment, not an expense. Set aside a portion of your budget for marketing efforts each month or quarter, focusing on initiatives that align with your goals. A well-planned marketing budget can maximize your reach and drive growth.

### Key Takeaway: Marketing with Purpose and Consistency

Effective marketing connects with clients, builds brand awareness, and fosters loyalty. Approach it as a growth tool and be deliberate and consistent in sharing your message. With a strategic marketing plan, you'll increase your reach, establish credibility, and create a strong, lasting brand.

## Chapter 8 - Marketing Summary

*Effective marketing connects with clients, builds brand awareness, and fosters loyalty.*

# Chapter 9

## Human Resources

People are the heart of any organization. Building the right team is crucial, as your employees represent your brand and directly impact your business's reputation and success.

### Motivation and Finding the Right Fit

Hiring the right people means understanding what motivates them. During the interview process, ask questions to gauge alignment with your company's goals:

- "What excites you most about this role?"
- "How does this position fit into your personal career goals?"

These questions can reveal whether the candidate is passionate about the role or simply seeking a paycheck.

### Defining Roles and Qualities for Key Positions

Each position in your organization requires unique qualities.

For instance:

- Leadership Roles:
  Look for individuals with strong decision-making skills and the ability to inspire others.
- Customer-Facing Roles:
  Seek employees who are personable, reliable, and genuinely care about client satisfaction.
- Support Roles:
  Focus on individuals who are organized, efficient, and comfortable working behind the scenes.

### Fostering a Positive Work Culture

- Creating a positive, growth-oriented environment goes a long way in retaining talent. Consider these tips:

- Regular Feedback: Offer constructive feedback to help team members improve.

- Recognition: Acknowledge hard work and accomplishments.

- Skill Development: Encourage ongoing training and development opportunities.

### Building Team Loyalty

Investing in your team builds loyalty and reduces turnover. When employees see opportunities for growth and feel valued, they're more likely to stay committed and motivated to contribute to the company's success.

### Key Takeaway: People as Assets

Your team is an asset—treat them as such. By building an environment where employees feel valued, supported, and aligned with your vision, you'll create a loyal, high-performing team that propels your business forward.

## Chapter 9 - Human Resources Summary

*A positive environment supports your team and encourages growth.*

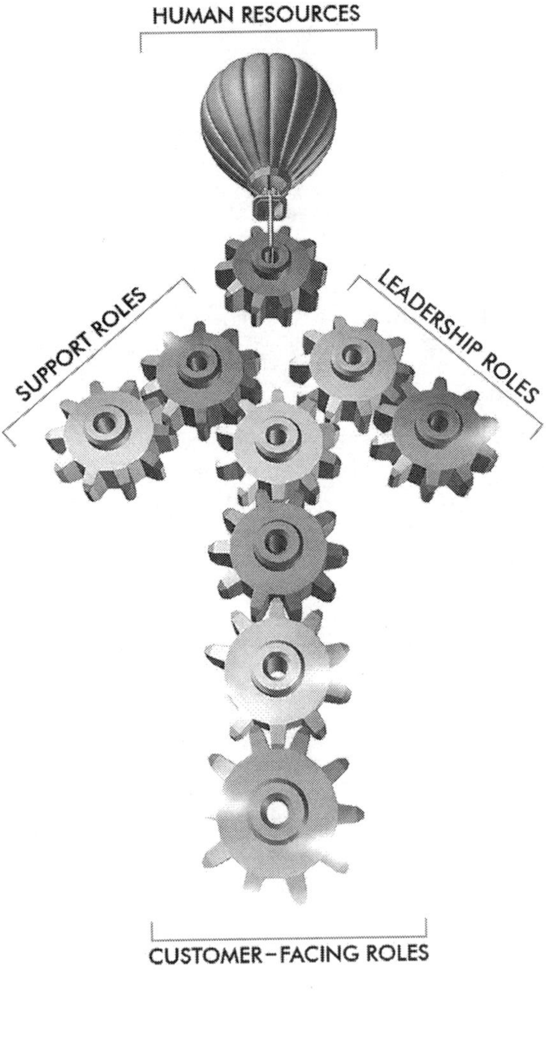

# Chapter 10

## Progressing with Passion

Passion is the fuel that sustains you through the "highs and lows" of entrepreneurship. It's the essential driving force that pushes you to keep going, even when obstacles arise. In this final chapter, we'll explore how to reconnect with your passion and use it to propel your business forward.

### Reflecting on the Role of Passion in Your Journey

For me, passion has been a constant, especially when challenges seem overwhelming. It's what kept me moving when giving up seemed easier. While reflecting on your own journey, remember the moments when passion kept you going—let those moments serve as a reminder of why you began this endeavor.

### Practical Passion Exercise

Use this exercise to reconnect with your "why" and ignite your passion:

- Remember Your Motivation: Write down what inspired you to start this journey.
- Identify What You Love Most: List three things you enjoy most about your work.
- Visualize the Impact: Think about the positive impact your business has on clients and the community.

### Examples of Passion-Driven Success

Successful entrepreneurs often credit passion for their resilience. Whether it's overcoming initial failures or adapting to change, passion has carried countless leaders through their toughest moments. Let these stories inspire you to harness your own passion and stay committed to your journey.

### Key Takeaway: Passion as a Compass

Passion isn't just about excitement; it's also about perseverance, adaptability, and commitment. It's the foundation that keeps you grounded in your purpose. As you move forward, let passion guide your decisions, fuel your resilience, and remind you that you're here to create something meaningful.

### Summary: Embracing the Entrepreneurial Journey

10 Rules to Entrepreneurship: Answer Your Call, Live Your Dream is more than a guide—it's a call to action for those ready to step into their purpose. This journey to entrepreneurship demands more than just a business plan or a location. It calls for resilience, adaptability, and a willingness to grow at every stage. Each rule presented here reflects a core principle for building a business that doesn't just serve clients, but also fulfills a personal calling.

### What This Journey Requires

Success as an entrepreneur requires vision, faith, and the courage to pursue your path, even when it diverges from what feels safe or familiar. It's about embracing flexibility in your business plan, and creating a brand that resonates with others. This venture entails finding the right partners and team members to bring your vision to life.

### Building a Strong Foundation

Every step—whether securing capital, selecting a location, or establishing a marketing strategy—is a piece of a larger puzzle. These aren't just tasks; they're building blocks that form the foundation of your dream. When each piece aligns with your values and purpose, the result is a business that stands the test of time and makes a lasting impact on your life, as well as your community.

### Passion as the Driving Force

At the heart of this journey lies passion! It's the unwavering force that will keep you moving forward, pushing through obstacles and celebrating each milestone. Passion isn't just an emotion—it's a commitment to excellence and a desire to bring your vision into the world.

### Closing Call to Action

As you close this book, I encourage you to take each rule to heart. Let them guide you, challenge you, and strengthen your resolve. The road won't always be easy, but remember why you started. You're here to live your dream with purpose, resilience, and an unshakeable belief in your vision. Answer your call, stay true to your journey, and let your dream unfold.

**Chapter 10 - Progressing with Passion Summary**

*Allow your passion (what you love most) —*
*to be your guiding compass.*

MOTIVATION + WHAT YOU LOVE MOST + IMPACT
= RESILENCE